THIS BOOK BELONGS TO

_____

Amazing Grace

PRAYERS & PROMISES *for Women*

BroadStreet
PUBLISHING

CONTENTS

Acceptance	4	Honor	74
Anger	6	Hope	76
Anxiety	8	Humility	78
Beauty	10	Inspiration	80
Blessings	12	Integrity	82
Boldness	14	Joy	84
Caring	16	Justice	86
Change	18	Kindness	88
Compassion	20	Life	90
Confidence	22	Light	92
Contentment	24	Loneliness	94
Courage	26	Loss	96
Courtesy	28	Love	98
Creativity	30	Patience	100
Delight	32	Peace	102
Depression	34	Perseverance	104
Devotion	36	Praise	106
Encouragement	38	Prayer	108
Eternity	40	Protection	110
Excellence	42	Purpose	112
Faith	44	Reliability	114
Faithfulness	46	Respect	116
Fear	48	Reward	118
Forgiveness	50	Salvation	120
Freedom	52	Serving	122
Friendship	54	Strength	124
Generosity	56	Stress	126
Gentleness	58	Temptation	128
Goodness	60	Thankfulness	130
Grace	62	Trust	132
Guidance	64	Truth	134
Guilt	66	Understanding	136
Health	68	Victory	138
Helpfulness	70	Wisdom	140
Honesty	72	Worry	142

Introduction

It is a wonderful blessing to be a daughter of God! You can take great joy in knowing that he made you special and he desires a close relationship with you. Spending time in his Word each day will fill you with hope and peace.

Amazing Grace: Prayers & Promises for Women is a topically organized collection that guides you through lessons of beauty, confidence, love, joy, wisdom, and more. Heartfelt prayers and prompting questions give you an opportunity to think more deeply about the promises found in God's Word.

Be encouraged and strengthened as you dwell on the faithfulness of God.

Acceptance

"The Father gives me the people who are mine.
Every one of them will come to me,
and I will always accept them."

JOHN 6:37 NCV

The LORD does not see as man sees;
for man looks at the outward appearance,
but the LORD looks at the heart.

1 SAMUEL 16:7 NKJV

If God is for us, who can be against us?

ROMANS 8:31 ESV

Before he made the world, God chose us to be his very
own through what Christ would do for us; he decided
then to make us holy in his eyes, without a single fault—
we who stand before him covered with his love.

EPHESIANS 1:4 TLB

Like the perfect Father you are, you accept me as I am.
You have decided that I am worthy through your Son.
All are worthy who choose to believe. All are welcome.
As this acceptance is in your heart, let it be in mine.

*How does God's acceptance of you help
you be more accepting of others?*

Anger

Don't get angry.
Don't be upset; it only leads to trouble.
Evil people will be sent away,
but those who trust the LORD will inherit the land.

PSALM 37:8-9 NCV

Everyone should be quick to listen, slow to speak
and slow to become angry, because human anger
does not produce the righteousness that God desires.

JAMES 1:19-20 NIV

"Don't sin by letting anger control you."
Don't let the sun go down while you are still angry.

EPHESIANS 4:26 NLT

Lord, your Word tells me you are slow to anger. I cannot always say the same of myself. I confess there are plenty of days where I move the wrong way—a harsh word, a hasty action, and sometimes I hold onto my anger for the rest of the day. I don't want to be like this. When I feel anger rising, Lord, let your love and forgiveness rise faster.

What does it mean to be quick to listen and slow to speak?

Anxiety

You will keep in perfect peace those whose minds
are steadfast, because they trust in you.

ISAIAH 26:3 NIV

"Don't let your hearts be troubled. Trust in God,
and trust also in me."

JOHN 14:1 NLT

Give all your worries to him,
because he cares about you.

1 PETER 5:7 NCV

I call out to the LORD when I'm in trouble,
and he answers me.

PSALM 120:1 NIRV

Lord, I get anxious about the future. I try to imagine it, and it seems so vague and uncertain; all blurry around the edges. Forgive my anxiety. I don't want to dishonor you, and I do trust you with my life. I give you my worries and cares and leave them with you, knowing that it does no good for me to control them myself.

What steps can you take to be less anxious and more trusting?

Beauty

You are altogether beautiful, my darling,
beautiful in every way.

Song of Songs 4:7 nlt

No, your beauty should come from within you—
the beauty of a gentle and quiet spirit that will never
be destroyed and is very precious to God.

1 Peter 3:4 ncv

She puts on strength and honor
as if they were her clothes.
She can laugh at the days that are coming.

Proverbs 31:25 nirv

I praise you because you made me
in an amazing and wonderful way.
What you have done is wonderful. I know this very well.

Psalm 139:14 ncv

God, you make beautiful things! Thank you for
a lovely world. I know that to those who love me, I add to
the world's beauty. This humbles me. In the mirror, I see
things I would like to change. Behind me, hands resting
proudly on my shoulders, your eyes see your beautiful,
beloved daughter. To you, I am more beautiful than
the sunset. I am as lovely as a rose.

*How does it make you feel to think God
sees you as beautiful?*

Blessings

Surely, Lord, you bless those who do what is right.
Like a shield, your loving care keeps them safe.

Psalm 5:12 NIRV

Surely you have granted him unending blessings
and made him glad with the joy of your presence.

Psalm 21:6 NIV

"Even more blessed are all who hear the word of God
and put it into practice."

Luke 11:28 NLT

Give praise to the God and Father of our Lord Jesus
Christ. He has blessed us with every spiritual blessing.
Those blessings come from the heavenly world. They
belong to us because we belong to Christ. God chose us to
belong to Christ before the world was created. He chose
us to be holy and without blame in his eyes. He loved us.

Ephesians 1:3-4 NIRV

God, how much fun you must have, dreaming up blessings to rain down on your children. Your affection for me is not subject to my behavior toward you. You continue to fix your thoughts on me even when I selfishly ignore your blessings. Help me to see all that you have blessed me with today.

Which of God's blessings come to your mind today?

Boldness

He proclaimed the kingdom of God and taught
about the Lord Jesus Christ—with all boldness
and without hindrance!

ACTS 28:31 NIV

Sinners run away even when no one is chasing them.
But those who do what is right are as bold as lions.

PROVERBS 28:1 NIRV

On the day I called you, you answered me.
You made me strong and brave.

PSALM 138:3 NCV

Let us come boldly to the throne of our gracious God.
There we will receive his mercy, and we will find grace
to help us when we need it most.

HEBREWS 4:16 NLT

Creator God, what is beyond your capability? What task are you unqualified for? When I feel overwhelmed and incapable, help me remember I don't need to panic. We are in this together, and your awesomeness more than makes up for my shortcoming. When I lack confidence, let me find it in you. Infuse me with your ability to be bold. If this work I do is for you, I cannot fail.

Why is it sometimes hard to be bold?

Caring

Do not be interested only in your own life,
but be interested in the lives of others.

PHILIPPIANS 2:4 NCV

If anyone has material possessions and sees a brother
or sister in need but has no pity on them, how can the
love of God be in that person? Dear children, let us not
love with words or speech but with actions and in truth.

1 JOHN 3:17–18 NIV

"I was hungry. And you gave me something to eat.
I was thirsty. And you gave me something to drink.
I was a stranger. And you invited me in. I needed
clothes. And you gave them to me. I was sick. And you
took care of me. I was in prison. And you came to visit
me. …The King will reply, 'What I'm about to tell you
is true. Anything you did for one of the least important
of these brothers and sisters of mine, you did for me.'"

MATTHEW 25:35–36, 40 NIRV

God, that you would choose to share my life, all the highs and lows, is such a miracle to me. To know you hurt when I'm hurting, and you laugh when I'm laughing just does me in. How can I matter so much to you? Open my heart to the blessing of empathy, so I can laugh and cry with others in their joy and pain.

How can you care
for someone else today?

Change

Look! I tell you this secret:
We will not all sleep in death,
but we will all be changed.

1 CORINTHIANS 15:51 NCV

He will take our weak mortal bodies and change them
into glorious bodies like his own, using the same power
with which he will bring everything under his control.

PHILIPPIANS 3:21 NLT

Jesus Christ is the same yesterday and today and forever.

HEBREWS 13:8 NIRV

Our faces, then, are not covered. We all show the Lord's
glory, and we are being changed to be like him. This
change in us brings ever greater glory, which comes from
the Lord, who is the Spirit.

2 CORINTHIANS 3:18 NCV

Unchanging Lord, how intriguing that you created a world where nothing stays the same. Only you are perfect so everything else must change. The color of the sky changes minute to minute, and even the hardest of rocks wear down with time. Perhaps most striking of all, I am never the same person upon rising as I was the day before. Let all my growth and change be toward becoming more like you, and help me not to be rattled by things that change around me, knowing that you remain the same.

How do you handle change?

Compassion

When I am with those who are weak, I share their
weakness, for I want to bring the weak to Christ.
Yes, I try to find common ground with everyone,
doing everything I can to save some.

1 CORINTHIANS 9:22 NLT

God, have mercy on me according to your faithful love.
Because your love is so tender and kind,
wipe out my lawless acts.

PSALM 51:1 NIRV

Praise be to the God and Father of our Lord Jesus Christ,
the Father of compassion and the God of all comfort.

2 CORINTHIANS 1:3 NIV

Merciful Lord, you see my desperation and you cannot stay where you are. You long to intercede. A soon as I ask, you respond. Compassion moves you. Move me, Lord! Show me something that breaks your heart, and let it break mine. Let the pain I feel for others pluck me from my comfort and place me right in the middle of their suffering, ready, willing, and even desperate to act.

How can you be a more compassionate person?

Confidence

I can do everything through Christ,
who gives me strength.

PHILIPPIANS 4:13 NLT

Be my rock of refuge,
to which I can always go;
give the command to save me,
for you are my rock and my fortress....
For You have been my hope, Sovereign LORD,
my confidence since my youth.

PSALM 71:3, 5 NIV

Do not throw away your confidence,
which has a great reward.

HEBREWS 10:35 NCV

Help me to remember, God, that I can approach your throne with confidence. You love it when I spend time with you. Knowing this gives me strength to hold my head high and face each day without wavering. You are my confidence.

How do you find your confidence?

Contentment

To enjoy your work and to accept your lot in life—
that is indeed a gift from God. The person who does
that will not need to look back with sorrow on his past,
for God gives him joy.

ECCLESIASTES 5:20 TLB

I know what it is to be in need, and I know what it is to
have plenty. I have learned the secret of being content
in any and every situation, whether well fed or hungry,
whether living in plenty or in want. I can do all this
through him who gives me strength.

PHILIPPIANS 4:12-13 NIV

*God of contentment, you bring me such peace. I forget
this sometimes when my situation becomes difficult; I take
my eyes off you, where perfect peace resides, and I focus all
my attention on the problem. This brings the opposite of
contentment and is not at all how I wish to live. Allow me to
rest in the knowledge that you are good and all will be well.*

How can you choose to be content
with your life as it is right now?

Courage

Be strong in the Lord and in his mighty power.
Put on the full armor of God, so that you can take your
stand against the devil's schemes.

EPHESIANS 6:10-11 NIV

Be alert. Continue strong in the faith. Have courage,
and be strong. Do everything in love.

1 CORINTHIANS 16:13-14 NCV

Even though I walk through the darkest valley,
I will not be afraid. You are with me.
Your shepherd's rod and staff comfort me.

PSALM 23:4 NIRV

"This is my command—be strong and courageous!
Do not be afraid or discouraged. For the LORD your God
is with you wherever you go."

JOSHUA 1:9 NLT

God who supplies all courage, I feel like I keep coming back to this well again and again. How grateful I am for your endless supply of courage. How I'd be lost without it. I am so encouraged by your presence. With you, I can face anything; I have nothing to fear.

When was the last time you asked God for courage?

Courtesy

Each of us should please our neighbors for their good,
to build them up. For even Christ did not please himself
but, as it is written: "The insults of those who insult you
have fallen on me."

ROMANS 15:2-3 NIV

Welcome strangers, because some who have done
this have welcomed angels without knowing it.

HEBREWS 13:2 NCV

Remind God's people to obey rulers and authorities.
Remind them to be ready to do what is good. Tell them
not to speak evil things against anyone. Remind them to
live in peace. They must consider the needs of others.
They must always be gentle toward everyone.

TITUS 3:1-2 NIRV

Lord, your words are beautiful, life giving, and inspiring. I wish all of mine were the same. Please mend the hearts I've hurt with my words, including my own. When unkindness or criticism tries to leave my mouth, let it be caught in my throat. Then fill me with words that give life, and a desire to share those words with others.

Why isn't it easy to put others'
needs before your own?

Creativity

LORD, you have made many things;
with your wisdom you made them all.
The earth is full of your riches.

PSALM 104:24 NCV

We are God's masterpiece. He has created us anew
in Christ Jesus, so we can do the good things
he planned for us long ago.

EPHESIANS 2:10 NLT

The Lord has filled him with the Spirit of God.
He has filled him with wisdom, with understanding,
with knowledge and with all kinds of skill.

EXODUS 35:31 NIRV

We have different gifts, according
to the grace given to each of us.

ROMANS 12:6 NIV

Lord, you made the world so beautiful, interesting, and exciting. You made people so unique and lovable, work so rewarding, and play so much fun. Please help me appreciate your creation and recognize that you have given me the ability to be creative as well. I want to use my creativity for your glory.

How can you use your creativity for God?

Delight

When I received your words, I ate them.
They filled me with joy. My heart took delight in them.
Lord God who rules over all, I belong to you.

Jeremiah 15:16 NIRV

My God, I want to do what you want.
Your teachings are in my heart.

Psalm 40:8 NCV

Your laws are my treasure;
they are my heart's delight.

Psalm 119:111 NLT

"Let your light shine before others, that they may see
your good deeds and glorify your Father in heaven."

Matthew 5:16 NIV

God of the universe, how is it that I matter to you? I think of my mark here—how small and insignificant—and it just astonishes me that you count me so precious. The significance you give me by caring so deeply inspires me to live a life of greater meaning. Your delight in me is unexplainable, and I am so grateful.

How hard is it for you to fathom God's incredible delight in you?

Depression

The LORD hears his people when they call to him for help.
He rescues them from all their troubles.

PSALM 34:17 NLT

Why am I so sad?
Why am I so upset?
I should put my hope in God
and keep praising him.

PSALM 42:11 NCV

You, O LORD, are a shield about me, my glory,
and the lifter of my head.

PSALM 3:3 ESV

He has delivered us from the power of darkness and
conveyed us into the kingdom of the Son of His love.

COLOSSIANS 1:13 NKJV

Father, there are days I just want to crawl into your lap and stay. When those days string together and I find myself brought low, it comforts me to know you see my sadness, and you want nothing more than to take it from me. You don't consider me ungrateful or selfish on these days; you just love me. Thank you for the shelter of your arms, the comfort of your embrace, and the deliverance of your joy.

Can you sense God's comfort and joy in the middle of your sadness today?

Devotion

Then Jesus said to his disciples, "Whoever wants
to be my disciple must deny themselves
and take up their cross and follow me."

MATTHEW 16:24 NIV

"No servant can serve two masters. The servant will hate
one master and love the other, or will follow one master
and refuse to follow the other. You cannot serve both
God and worldly riches."

LUKE 16:13 NCV

Don't copy the behavior and customs of this world,
but let God transform you into a new person by changing
the way you think. Then you will learn to know God's
will for you, which is good and pleasing and perfect.

ROMANS 12:2 NLT

God, I belong to you. I adore you, and I want to live my life fully committed to you. Knowing Jesus laid down his perfect life for me, I want only to honor his sacrifice by doing the same. Because I am weak, I know that even though I want this I can't do it without your help. Strengthen me, God, to live my life for you. I surrender all I am and all I have to your will.

How can you devote your life more to God?

Encouragement

The LORD your God is with you;
the mighty One will save you.
He will rejoice over you.
You will rest in his love;
he will sing and be joyful about you.

ZEPHANIAH 3:17 NCV

Encourage one another daily,
as long as it is called "Today."

HEBREWS 3:13 NIV

Be joyful. Grow to maturity.
Encourage each other.
Live in harmony and peace.
Then the God of love and peace
will be with you.

2 CORINTHIANS 13:11 NLT

God, your Word brings so much encouragement! No matter what I am up against, there is a source of strength, comfort, and wisdom. Because of all you've done for me, I find myself wanting to share it and be an encouragement to those around me. Let me be a resource of hope as I point others to you.

How can you encourage someone today?

Eternity

We are citizens of heaven, where the Lord Jesus Christ
lives. And we are eagerly waiting for him to return
as our Savior.

PHILIPPIANS 3:20 NLT

"And if I go and prepare a place for you,
I will come back and take you to be with me
that you also may be where I am."

JOHN 14:3 NIV

That will happen in a flash, as quickly as you can wink
an eye. It will happen at the blast of the last trumpet.
Then the dead will be raised to live forever.
And we will be changed.

1 CORINTHIANS 15:52 NIRV

Surely your goodness and love will be with me all my life,
and I will live in the house of the Lord forever.

PSALM 23:6 NCV

Eternal Lord, I think of the whole span of my life, eternity as I know it, and know it's just the tiniest fraction of time to you. It's hard to grasp, and to be honest, I'm not even sure I want to comprehend it. Though I cannot understand it, my heart knows it will be fully satisfied with you because you are good and absolutely perfect. You would not intend something that wasn't utterly wonderful.

Can you view eternity with a hopeful, happy heart, fully trusting in a good God?

Excellence

Finally, my brothers and sisters, always think about
what is true. Think about what is noble, right and pure.
Think about what is lovely and worthy of respect.
If anything is excellent or worthy of praise,
think about those kinds of things.

PHILIPPIANS 4:8 NIRV

By his divine power, God has given us everything we
need for living a godly life. We have received all of this
by coming to know him, the one who called us to himself
by means of his marvelous glory and excellence.

2 PETER 1:3 NLT

The answer is, if you eat or drink, or if you do anything,
do it all for the glory of God.

1 CORINTHIANS 10:31 NCV

Father, I know you don't need me, but I pray you will use me. I want to achieve great things in your name. I'm excited about the purpose you have given me, and I want to serve you and bring you glory. Plant your Word in my heart and empower me with the ability to reflect your goodness and your excellence in everything you ask me to do.

In which areas would you like to be excellent for God?

Faith

Through Christ you have come to trust in God.
And you have placed your faith and hope in God because
he raised Christ from the dead and gave him great glory.

1 PETER 1:21 NLT

"Because your faith is much too small. What I'm about
to tell you is true. If you have faith as small as a mustard
seed, it is enough. You can say to this mountain,
'Move from here to there.' And it will move.
Nothing will be impossible for you."

MATTHEW 17:20 NIRV

The important thing is faith—
the kind of faith that works through love.

GALATIANS 5:6 NCV

Faith is confidence in what we hope
for and assurance about what we do not see.

HEBREWS 11:1 NIV

All-powerful God, nothing is beyond your ability, no matter how audacious. And no matter how simple, no sincere prayer is unworthy of your consideration. You delight in answering our faithful prayers. I ask you for a heart filled to overflowing with faith that will not doubt your response.

What gives you faith and hope in Jesus?

Faithfulness

Your lovingkindness, O LORD, extends to the heavens,
Your faithfulness reaches to the skies.

PSALM 36:5 NASB

The Lord is faithful, who will establish you
and guard you from the evil one.

2 THESSALONIANS 3:3 NKJV

LORD, you are my God; I will exalt you and praise
your name, for in perfect faithfulness you have done
wonderful things, things planned long ago.

ISAIAH 25:1 NIV

The word of the LORD is upright,
and all his work is done in faithfulness.

PSALM 33:4 ESV

Faithful God. I just want to stop for a moment and consider what that means—faithful God. You are the perfect one, the one who deserves all of my devotion; yet, you are committed to me, no matter how many times I let you down. There is no end to your awesomeness, and daily I benefit.

How have you seen the faithfulness of God played out in your life?

Fear

God gave us his Spirit. And the Spirit doesn't make
us weak and fearful. Instead, the Spirit gives us power
and love. He helps us control ourselves.

2 TIMOTHY 1:7 NIRV

The LORD is my light and my salvation—
whom shall I fear?
The LORD is the stronghold of my life—
of whom shall I be afraid?

PSALM 27:1 NIV

When I am afraid, I will trust you.
I praise God for his word.
I trust God, so I am not afraid.
What can human beings do to me?

PSALM 56:3-4 NCV

Faithful God, with you I have no need of fear. Yet still I struggle with it. Fear feels like a living thing. It comes in and takes hold of my thoughts, lying to me and trying to convince me I can't rely on you to save me. But you are near. I only need to speak your name and fear retreats. Thank you, Jesus, for the saving power of your name.

What fears can you give to God right now?

Forgiveness

"If you forgive other people when they sin against you,
your heavenly Father will also forgive you."

MATTHEW 6:14 NIV

Put up with each other. Forgive one another
if you are holding something against someone.
Forgive, just as the Lord forgave you.

COLOSSIANS 3:13 NIRV

God is faithful and fair. If we confess our sins,
he will forgive our sins. He will forgive every wrong
thing we have done. He will make us pure.

1 JOHN 1:9 NIRV

He is so rich in kindness and grace that he purchased our
freedom with the blood of his Son and forgave our sins.

EPHESIANS 1:7 NLT

Sinless, perfect Lord, you've forgiven every wrong I've ever committed. With a heart so open to forgiveness, how it must grieve you when I hold onto a grudge or nurse my anger. Will you help me? Help me to forgive, that I may be forgiven.

Who might you need to extend forgiveness to today?

Freedom

Now the Lord is the Spirit, and where the Spirit
of the Lord is, there is freedom.

2 CORINTHIANS 3:17 NIV

My brothers and sisters, you were chosen to be free.
But don't use your freedom as an excuse to live under
the power of sin. Instead, serve one another in love.

GALATIANS 5:13 NIRV

"So if the Son sets you free, you are truly free."

JOHN 8:36 NLT

We have freedom now, because Christ made us free.
So stand strong. Do not change and go back
into the slavery of the law.

GALATIANS 5:1 NCV

God, you set captives free. When I become ensnared, you
offer a way out. Your redeeming grace opens the door to my
jail cell, and you call me into the freedom of your love. Thank
you for pulling me out of the darkness and being patient with
me as I become accustomed to the light.

How does it feel to be free from your sin?

Friendship

A friend loves you all the time,
and a brother helps in time of trouble.

PROVERBS 17:17 NCV

There are "friends" who destroy each other,
but a real friend sticks closer than a brother.

PROVERBS 18:24 NLT

"Greater love has no one than this: to lay down
one's life for one's friends. You are my friends
if you do what I command…. Instead,
I have called you friends, for everything that I learned
from my Father I have made known to you."

JOHN 15:13-15 NIV

"In everything, do to others what you
would want them to do to you."

MATTHEW 7:12 NIRV

God, you are such a faithful friend. No one could care more about me than you do. I know you designed us for relationships, and I long to be around people—especially people who love you. Lead me into relationships that encourage me to be more like you. Please continue to enrich my life with good friends.

What friends spur you on in your relationship with God?

Generosity

Give generously to them and do so without a grudging
heart; then because of this the LORD your God will bless you
in all your work and in everything you put your hand to.

DEUTERONOMY 15:10 NIV

Each of you should give what you have decided in your
heart to give. You shouldn't give if you don't want to.
You shouldn't give because you are forced to.
God loves a cheerful giver.

2 CORINTHIANS 9:7 NIRV

If you help the poor, you are lending to the Lord—
and he will repay you!

PROVERBS 19:17 NLT

You are so generous, Lord! When I give generously, your blessing pours back to me. Not only does your joy fill my heart but you replace what I give away. Though I know this to be true, I confess I don't always want to give. Don't let those selfish impulses win! Move me to share all that's mine. It is more than I can hold anyway.

How do you feel when
you share with others?

Gentleness

"Accept my teachings and learn from me,
because I am gentle and humble in spirit,
and you will find rest for your lives."

MATTHEW 11:29 NCV

"Blessed are those who are humble.
They will be given the earth."

MATTHEW 5:5 NIRV

A gentle answer turns away wrath,
but a harsh word stirs up anger.

PROVERBS 15:1 NIV

Some people have gone astray without knowing it.
He is able to deal gently with them.

HEBREWS 5:2 NIRV

Gentle Father, your patience and tenderness are so much more than I can fathom. I want to be more gentle with my words and actions. Fill me with a gentleness that defies my circumstances so I can reflect your loving attitude no matter what comes my way.

What are some steps you can take to become more gentle?

Goodness

Everything God created is good, and nothing
is to be rejected if it is received with thanksgiving.

1 TIMOTHY 4:4 NIV

Taste and see that the LORD is good.
Oh, the joys of those who take refuge in him!

PSALM 34:8 NLT

My brothers and sisters, I am sure that you are full
of goodness. I know that you have all the knowledge
you need and that you are able to teach each other.

ROMANS 15:14 NCV

Lord, thank you for your goodness and for the assurance in your Word that with you as my shepherd, goodness follows me wherever I go. What a beautiful image—being pursued by goodness. My prayer today is that I would slow down enough to be overrun by your goodness.

Where do you see the goodness of God the most in your life?

Grace

From his fullness we have all received, grace upon grace.

JOHN 1:16 NRSV

God gives us even more grace,
as the Scripture says,
"God is against the proud,
but he gives grace to the humble."

JAMES 4:6 NCV

Sin is no longer your master, for you no longer live
under the requirements of the law. Instead, you live
under the freedom of God's grace.

ROMANS 6:14 NLT

God saved you by his grace when you believed.
And you can't take credit for this; it is a gift from God.

EPHESIANS 2:8 NLT

God, how do I begin to thank you for your grace? By definition, I am unworthy, and I daily prove this to be true. Impossibly, you love me no matter what I do, and I don't even have to ask. Before I even know I need it, it's already given. I am overwhelmed by your grace. Thank you.

What does God's grace look like in your life?

Guidance

Guide me in your truth and teach me,
for you are God my Savior,
and my hope is in you all day long.

PSALM 25:5 NIV

Wise people can also listen and learn;
even they can find good advice in these words.

PROVERBS 1:5 NCV

We can make our plans,
but the LORD determines our steps.

PROVERBS 16:9 NLT

Those who are led by the Spirit of God
are children of God.

ROMANS 8:14 NIRV

God, how wonderful it is to follow you! I don't have to know where I'm going or worry about leading anyone on the wrong path. There is such freedom in knowing that you know exactly where I need to go, and you will do everything necessary to get me there. Help me follow you willingly, so that anyone looking to me for direction will not miss you either.

Is there anything God can help guide you in today?

Guilt

God is faithful and fair. If we confess our sins,
he will forgive our sins. He will forgive every
wrong thing we have done. He will make us pure.

1 JOHN 1:9 NIRV

The LORD and King helps me. He won't let me
be dishonored. So I've made up my mind to keep on
serving him. I know he won't let me be put to shame.

ISAIAH 50:7 NIRV

Those who go to him for help are happy,
and they are never disgraced.

PSALM 34:5 NCV

I have not achieved it, but I focus on this one thing:
Forgetting the past and looking forward to what lies
ahead.

PHILIPPIANS 3:13 NLT

God of peace, how do I accept what I do not deserve?
Though I am guilty of many things, you release me from all
of them. You send my shame to the bottom of the ocean.
You separate me from my guilt as the east is from the west.
Thank you, Father. You are so very good.

Why doesn't God want you to feel guilt and shame?

Health

The world and its desires pass away,
but whoever does the will of God lives forever.

1 JOHN 2:17 NIV

Don't be wise in your own eyes.
Have respect for the Lord and avoid evil.
That will bring health to your body.
It will make your bones strong.

PROVERBS 3:7-8 NIRV

I will never forget your commandments,
for by them you give me life.

PSALM 119:93 NLT

A happy heart is like good medicine,
but a broken spirit drains your strength.

PROVERBS 17:22 NCV

Healer, I need you! I know what you can do; I've read it and I've seen it. Today, I claim your healing. You know my need. The brokenness in body and spirit for which I pray is not news to you. You are intimately involved, waiting to intercede. I believe you, Lord. I know you can heal me. Boldly I ask for that healing today.

What healing are you believing God for right now?

Helpfulness

In everything I did, I showed you that by this kind
of hard work we must help the weak, remembering
the words the Lord Jesus himself said: It is more
blessed to give than to receive.

ACTS 20:35 NIV

"Who is more important? Is it the one at the table,
or the one who serves? Isn't it the one who is at the
table? But I am among you as one who serves."

LUKE 22:27 NIRV

Share with God's people who need help.
Bring strangers in need into your homes.

ROMANS 12:13 NCV

Give generously, for your gifts will return to you later.
Divide your gifts among many, for in the days ahead
you yourself may need much help.

ECCLESIASTES 11:1 -2 TLB

Ever-present God, you are over, under, around, and through all who call you Lord. This connection to you connects us to one another. Give me the joy of my brother, the heartache of my sister, and the confusion of my friend. Allow me to stand with them in complete agreement, and to meet with you there. Help me to feel what you feel for people and extend your helping hand where I can.

What is something helpful you could do for someone today?

Honesty

Keep me from deceitful ways;
be gracious to me and teach me your law.
I have chosen the way of faithfulness;
I have set my heart on your laws.

PSALM 119:29-30 NIV

"Everything that is hidden will become clear,
and every secret thing will be made known."

LUKE 8:17 NCV

The king is pleased with words from righteous lips;
he loves those who speak honestly.

PROVERBS 16:13 NLT

Instead, we will speak the truth in love.
So we will grow up in every way to become
the body of Christ. Christ is the head of the body.

EPHESIANS 4:15 NIRV

God, there is no deceit in you. You never try to trick me or mislead me, and your only true enemy is called the father of lies. I hate lies, yet I struggle with lying at times. Forgive my lies and make me brave enough to tell the truth. Even when it might hurt, remind me that lies hurt worse.

Is there anything you need to be honest about now?

Honor

"My Father will honor the one who serves me."

JOHN 12:26 NIV

Humble yourselves under the mighty power of God,
and at the right time he will lift you up in honor.

1 PETER 5:6 NLT

Anyone who wants to be godly and loving
finds life, success and honor.

PROVERBS 21:21 NIRV

Love each other like brothers and sisters. Give each
other more honor than you want for yourselves.

ROMANS 12:10 NCV

*God, in everything I do, I seek to honor you. I know
I don't always do a great job of it. I want all of my work,
my efforts, my accomplishments to give glory to you. And in
my failure, let me be honoring as well. Help me to accept my
shortcomings with humility and give you glory in everything.*

What does it mean to honor God in everything you do?

Hope

The LORD is good to those whose hope is in him,
to the one who seeks him.

LAMENTATIONS 3:25 NIV

Hope will never bring us shame. That's because God's
love has poured into our hearts. This happened through
the Holy Spirit, who has been given to us.

ROMANS 5:5 NIRV

The LORD's delight is in those who fear him,
those who put their hope in his unfailing love.

PSALM 147:11 NLT

May the God of hope fill you with all joy and peace
as you trust in him, so that you may overflow with hope
by the power of the Holy Spirit.

ROMANS 15:13 NIV

God, because I can trust you, I can believe for a good outcome in any situation. I am filled with hope as I await your answer, your solution, your response to my needs. Your promise turns impatience into expectation, and waiting into joy. Thank you for your gift of hope that is alive in me.

Knowing that God always hears you, what can you be hopeful for?

Humility

"Didn't I make everything by my power? That is how all things were created," announces the Lord. "The people I value are not proud. They are sorry for the wrong things they have done. They have great respect for what I say."

ISAIAH 66:2 NIRV

Humble yourselves before the Lord,
and he will lift you up.

JAMES 4:10 NIV

Pride will ruin people, but those who are humble
will be honored.

PROVERBS 29:23 NCV

The LORD has told you what is good,
and this is what he requires of you:
to do what is right, to love mercy,
and to walk humbly with your God.

MICAH 6:8 NLT

Father, your rewards are so generous, and by comparison, your demands are small. You desire humility, and in exchange you promise exaltation. Thank you for reminding me, through your own perfection, how very small I am and how much growing I have to do. Thank you for daily opportunities to earn your rich reward as I recognize my own limitations and learn to rely on your greatness.

What opportunities give you a chance to practice humility?

Inspiration

The precepts of the LORD are right,
giving joy to the heart.
The commands of the LORD are radiant,
giving light to the eyes.

PSALM 19:8 NIV

Your laws are my treasure;
they are my heart's delight.

PSALM 119:111 NLT

The whole Bible was given to us by inspiration from
God and is useful to teach us what is true and to make us
realize what is wrong in our lives; it straightens us out
and helps us do what is right.

2 TIMOTHY 3:16 TLB

Wonderful God, everywhere I look I see signs of your inventiveness, your playfulness, and your creativity. I take this beautiful world for granted at times. Will you inspire me today? Give me a fresh idea, a new perspective, an infusion of passion so that my work will be a delight to us both. Get me out of my rut, Lord, and tilt my chin upward to the dozen shades of blue in the sky above me. Inspire me, and then send me off to inspire others.

How do you find inspiration?

Integrity

I know, my God, that you test the heart and are pleased
with integrity. All these things I have given willingly
and with honest intent.

1 CHRONICLES 29:17 NIV

"So if you ignore the least commandment
and teach others to do the same, you will be called
the least in the Kingdom of Heaven. But anyone
who obeys God's laws and teaches them will be called
great in the Kingdom of Heaven."

MATTHEW 5:19 NLT

The honest person will live in safety,
but the dishonest will be caught.

PROVERBS 10:9 NCV

Father, you deserve nothing but my best. I offer you my love, my worship, my respect. I trust your plans for my life; I know your instructions are for my good and for your glory. I want to walk in integrity and obedience before you so that my love really looks like love and my worship comes from a place of truth.

Do you admire the integrity of someone in your life?

Joy

"I have told you this so that my joy may be in you
and that your joy may be complete."

JOHN 15:11 NIV

"Don't be sad, because the joy of the Lord
will make you strong."

NEHEMIAH 8:10 NCV

The LORD is my strength and shield.
I trust him with all my heart.
He helps me, and my heart is filled with joy.
I burst out in songs of thanksgiving.

PSALM 28:7 NLT

Always be joyful because you belong to the Lord.
I will say it again. Be joyful!

PHILIPPIANS 4:4 NIRV

Thank you, God, for joy. What a wonderful gift, to be truly glad no matter how things look or what situation I am in. In the middle of my deepest sorrow, you are there with your joy. Right at the center of a frustrating, stubborn problem, the joy of the Lord pops in with an inexplicable lightness and carries me home.

What is one truly joyful moment you've had recently?

Justice

My friends, do not try to punish others when they wrong
you, but wait for God to punish them with his anger.
It is written: "I will punish those who do wrong;
I will repay them," says the Lord.

ROMANS 12:19 NCV

He is the Rock. His works are perfect. All his ways are
right. He is faithful. He doesn't do anything wrong.
He is honest and fair.

DEUTERONOMY 32:4 NIRV

The LORD secures justice for the poor
and upholds the cause of the needy.

PSALM 140:12 NIV

There is joy for those who deal justly
with others and always do what is right.

PSALM 106:3 NLT

God, you are the only judge. Remind me of this as I am sinking under the weight of the opinions of others. Whether I'm being misunderstood or whether the assessment is accurate, remind me it is irrelevant. Only you get to decide who I am. Only you know my heart, Lord, and only you can change it. Help me to leave all my judgment with you.

Why is it better to let God be the judge?

Kindness

Be kind to each other, tenderhearted, forgiving one
another, just as God through Christ has forgiven you.

EPHESIANS 4:32 NLT

Kind people do themselves a favor,
but cruel people bring trouble on themselves.

PROVERBS 11:17 NCV

Do you disrespect God's great kindness and favor?
Do you disrespect God when he is patient with you?
Don't you realize that God's kindness is meant
to turn you away from your sins?

ROMANS 2:4 NIRV

For great is his love toward us,
and the faithfulness of the LORD endures forever.
Praise the LORD.

PSALM 117:2 NIV

God, in your great love, you took my cold, selfish heart and replaced it with warmth and compassion. Thank you for showing me how much there is to life. Thank you for feelings of mercy, grace, generosity, and kindness. Thank you for moments of completely forgetting myself as I am swept up in you. Thank you for opportunities to love others, people I would never have encountered before, and to point them to the source of my new radiance. Thank you for the new life of a kind heart.

*How can you extend kindness
to those around you today?*

Life

All praise to God, the Father of our Lord Jesus Christ.
It is by his great mercy that we have been born again,
because God raised Jesus Christ from the dead.
Now we live with great expectation.

1 PETER 1:3 NLT

That faith and that knowledge come
from the hope for life forever,
which God promised to us before time began.

TITUS 1:2 NCV

"I am the way and the truth and the life.
No one comes to the Father except through me."

JOHN 14:6 NIRV

God, thank you for the promise of forever life with you. You have blessed me with so many good things here in this life, and there is so much more to come! With every breath, I realize your mercy. I live because you desire life for me. Help me to glorify and honor you with my life.

What is your favorite part of life?

Light

"I am the light of the world. Whoever follows me will never walk in darkness, but will have the light of life."

JOHN 8:12 NIV

"You are the light of the world—like a city on a hilltop that cannot be hidden. No one lights a lamp and then puts it under a basket. Instead, a lamp is placed on a stand, where it gives light to everyone in the house. In the same way, let your good deeds shine out for all to see, so that everyone will praise your heavenly Father."

MATTHEW 5:14-16 NLT

At one time you were in the dark. But now you are in the light because of what the Lord has done. Live like children of the light.

EPHESIANS 5:8 NIRV

Jesus, thank you for your perfect example of how to live in the light. You inspire me to be a positive influence in my home and community. Help me to remember to keep my lamp on a stand, burning brightly, and encourage others to do the same. Let me live in a way that draws others to you. Let them see me and hear me and know that I am yours. Let my life bring you glory!

How can you let your light shine brightly today?

Loneliness

"Teach them to obey everything that I have taught you, and
I will be with you always, even until the end of this age."

MATTHEW 28:20 NCV

The LORD is near to all who call on him,
yes, to all who call on him in truth.

PSALM 145:18 NLT

Even if my father and mother abandon me,
the LORD will hold me close.

PSALM 27:10 NLT

"Be strong and courageous. Do not be afraid or terrified
because of them, for the LORD your God goes with you;
he will never leave you nor forsake you."

DEUTERONOMY 31:6 NIV

*How amazing it is to remember I am never alone! You
are my constant companion. You are always here to help,
guide, and comfort me. Only you can take away the ache of
aloneness, Lord. The closer I am walking with you, the fuller
my life becomes.*

When you feel lonely, can you turn
to God and ask him to surround you
with his presence?

Loss

Those who sow in tears shall reap with shouts of joy.

PSALM 126:5 ESV

Let your steadfast love become my comfort
according to your promise to your servant.

PSALM 119:76 NRSV

"Come to me, all you who are weary and burdened,
and I will give you rest. Take my yoke upon you and learn
from me, for I am gentle and humble in heart,
and you will find rest for your souls."

MATTHEW 11:28-29 NIV

Every valley shall be raised up,
every mountain and hill made low;
the rough ground shall become level,
the rugged places a plain.

ISAIAH 40:4 NIV

God, thank you for being constant. Loss leaving me feeling lost; grief is like a mountain with no discernible path. The way seems so unclear, the terrain unnavigable. I'm afraid if I raise my head, I'll fall right off the edge. But then I remember your promise, and I lift my eyes. You are here, right where you've always been, making a new way for me. Step by step, day by day, keep my eyes fixed on what I cannot lose. Thank you for your unchanging love.

Do you ask God for help when you need his comfort?

Love

Three things will last forever—faith, hope, and love—
and the greatest of these is love.

1 CORINTHIANS 13:13 NLT

LORD, you are good. You are forgiving.
You are full of love for all who call out to you.

PSALM 86:5 NIRV

Fill us with your love every morning.
Then we will sing and rejoice all our lives.

PSALM 90:14 NCV

Let love and faithfulness never leave you;
bind them around your neck,
write them on the tablet of your heart.

PROVERBS 3:3 NIV

Father God, nothing is more amazing than your love. The depth is so vast, I get lost in it—and what could be better? From this place, swimming in your love, it is easy to love others. Help me to love as you love: deeply without hesitation or thought of myself. Plunge me into your sea of love again and again, so I may love as you do.

How does the love of God in your life help you to love others?

Patience

Warn those who are lazy. Encourage those who are timid.
Take tender care of those who are weak.
Be patient with everyone.

1 THESSALONIANS 5:14 NLT

Be like those who through faith and patience
will receive what God has promised.

HEBREWS 6:12 NCV

Be completely humble and gentle;
be patient, bearing with one another in love.

EPHESIANS 4:2 NIV

Anyone who is patient has great understanding.
But anyone who gets angry quickly shows
how foolish they are.

PROVERBS 14:29 NIRV

God, waiting is hard! I look for the shortest lines in the grocery store, and the quickest-moving lane of traffic, and then I come to you and request the timeliest solutions to all my problems. When you don't answer right away, doubt creeps in. Fortify my heart with patience, courage, and strength while I wait for your perfect resolution. I trust your plan, and I rejoice in knowing all will be well.

*How can you show more patience
in your life?*

Peace

"I have told you these things, so that you can have peace
because of me. In this world you will have trouble. But be
encouraged! I have won the battle over the world."

JOHN 16:33 NIRV

The LORD gives his people strength.
The LORD blesses them with peace.

PSALM 29:11 NLT

May the Lord of peace himself give you peace at all times
and in every way. The Lord be with all of you.

2 THESSALONIANS 3:16 NIV

"I am leaving you with a gift—peace of mind and heart.
And the peace I give is a gift the world cannot give.
So don't be troubled or afraid."

JOHN 14:27 NLT

Lord of peace, thank you for being the source of this most precious and mysterious gift. Your peace renders me calm despite a raging storm of difficulty. Even when anxiety would seem to have a death grip on me, your peace draws me back to you. I am so grateful for your peace.

What does peace look like for you?

Perseverance

In a race all the runners run.
But only one gets the prize.
You know that, don't you?
So run in a way that will get you the prize.

1 CORINTHIANS 9:24–25 NIRV

I have tried hard to find you—
don't let me wander from your commands.

PSALM 119:10 NLT

I have fought the good fight, I have finished the race,
I have kept the faith.

2 TIMOTHY 4:7 NCV

Let us not become weary in doing good, for at the proper
time we will reap a harvest if we do not give up.

GALATIANS 6:9 NIV

*God, show me where I can be of use, and fill me with
an energy that doesn't fade—even when met with aching
muscles, competing desires, or ungrateful recipients. I know
you are there, in the midst of it all, and I don't want to miss
an opportunity to meet with you. Help me to persevere in all
you have called me to.*

What do you feel God is calling you to persevere in right now?

Praise

Praise the LORD from the skies.
Praise him high above the earth.
Praise him, all you angels.
Praise him, all you armies of heaven.
Praise him, sun and moon.
Praise him, all you shining stars.
Praise him, highest heavens
and you waters above the sky.
Let them praise the LORD,
because they were created by his command.

PSALM 148:1-5 NCV

God chose you to be his people. You are royal priests.
You are a holy nation. You are God's special treasure.
You are all these things so that you can give him praise.
God brought you out of darkness into his wonderful light.

1 PETER 2:9 NIRV

God, you are worthy. Praise, respect, honor, glory—all belong with you. With the help of your Spirit, let me find you in every good thing. Let all my worship be directed at you. Let me honor the author of my faith, glorify the inventor of glory, and praise the Father of goodness. You alone are worthy and I will worship you alone.

What is something specific you can praise God for today?

Prayer

LORD, in the morning you hear my voice.
In the morning I pray to you. I wait for you in hope.

PSALM 5:3 NIRV

Never stop praying.

1 THESSALONIANS 5:17 NIRV

The LORD does not listen to the wicked,
but he hears the prayers of those who do right.

PROVERBS 15:29 NCV

Come, let us bow down in worship,
let us kneel before the Lord our Maker;
for he is our God
and we are the people of his pasture,
the flock under his care.

PSALM 95:6-7 NIV

Lord Jesus, you promise to do whatever I ask in your name. Just to speak your name invites peace and confidence into my heart. You are always helping me, even when I don't get my way. To pray in your name is to pray surrendered to the Father, who is always working for my good. Thank you that my ultimate joy is always before you.

What can you pray about right now?

Protection

My God is my rock. I can run to him for safety.
He is my shield and my saving strength,
my defender and my place of safety.
The Lord saves me from those who want to harm me.

2 Samuel 22:3 ncv

The Lord keeps you from all harm
and watches over your life.
The Lord keeps watch over you as you come
and go, both now and forever.

Psalm 121:7-8 nlt

We are pushed hard from all sides. But we are not beaten
down. We are bewildered. But that doesn't make us lose
hope. Others make us suffer. But God does not desert us.
We are knocked down. But we are not knocked out.

2 Corinthians 4:8-9 nirv

Powerful God, what fight is too great for you? Nothing can defeat you: no scheme, no weapon—nothing. Though I know of your great power, I often try to fight my own battles. I don't want to play general today, God. I lay down my weapons, take shelter in your peace, and ask you to take over. Thank you for your protection.

How hard is it for you to lay down your battle plan and let God be your protector?

Purpose

For I know the plans I have for you," says the LORD.
"They are plans for good and not for disaster,
to give you a future and a hope."

JEREMIAH 29:11 NIV

We know that in all things God works for the good
of those who love him, who have been called
according to his purpose.

ROMANS 8:28 NIV

My child, pay attention to my words;
listen closely to what I say.
Don't ever forget my words;
keep them always in mind.

PROVERBS 4:20-21 NCV

Before I was even conceived, you thought of me. Lord of all creation, you spent time considering who I would be and what purpose I'd fulfill in your kingdom. I wonder how I can ever live up to the version of me you designed. I'm weak, flawed, so very human. But it doesn't depend on me, does it? My strength is from you. My gifts, talents, passions, and purpose are all from you. Today, I offer you my faith that if you willed it, I can fulfill it.

How do you feel when you think about God having a special purpose for your life?

Reliability

"All people are like grass. All their glory is like the
flowers in the field. The grass dries up. The flowers fall
to the ground. But the word of the LORD lasts forever."

1 PETER 1:24-25 NIRV

Every good action and every perfect gift is from God.
These good gifts come down from the Creator of the sun,
moon, and stars, who does not change
like their shifting shadows.

JAMES 1:17 NCV

You are near, LORD,
and all your commands are true.
Long ago I learned from your statutes
that you established them to last forever.

PSALM 119:151-152 NIV

Faithful God, your reliability is solid. I build my life on its foundation. If only my gratitude for your unwavering commitment to me gave me the same faithfulness toward others. Let me be dependable as you are dependable, committed as you are committed. Help me to be reliable and steady.

How does it make you feel to know you can rely on God for everything?

Respect

Show respect for all people: Love the brothers and sisters
of God's family, respect God, honor the king.

1 PETER 2:17 NCV

Trust in your leaders. Put yourselves under their
authority. Do this, because they keep watch over you.
They know they are accountable to God for everything
they do. Do this, so that their work will be a joy. If you
make their work a heavy load, it won't do you any good.

HEBREWS 13:17 NIRV

Acknowledge those who work hard among you,
who care for you in the Lord and who admonish you.
Hold them in the highest regard in love because
of their work. Live in peace with each other.

1 THESSALONIANS 5:12-13 NIV

God, nothing deserves more respect than you. We know to respect the power of the ocean or the storm, yet we fail to honor the one who made it, who tells it how far to go. You deserve all my respect, all my love, all my praise. I want to be a woman who respects you and all those you put in authority over me.

How do you show respect to the authority figures in your life?

Reward

Work willingly at whatever you do, as though you were
working for the Lord rather than for people. Remember
that the Lord will give you an inheritance as your reward,
and that the Master you are serving is Christ.

COLOSSIANS 3:23-24 NLT

"Love your enemies, do good to them, and lend to them
without expecting to get anything back. Then your
reward will be great, and you will be children of the Most
High, because he is kind to the ungrateful and wicked."

LUKE 6:35 NIV

Without faith it is impossible to please God. Those who
come to God must believe that he exists. And they must
believe that he rewards those who look to him.

HEBREWS 11:6 NIRV

God, even when I've lost hope in my circumstances and have no faith in my situation, thank you that I can always trust your purpose and your promises. When I get even just a glimpse of the reward that's coming, a peek at the beauty the future holds, all my hope is restored.

How does it make you feel knowing that God will reward you for your diligence?

Salvation

"This is how God loved the world: He gave his one
and only Son, so that everyone who believes in him
will not perish but have eternal life."

JOHN 3:16 NLT

For the wages of sin is death, but the gift of God
is eternal life in Christ Jesus our Lord.

ROMANS 6:23 NIV

God's grace has saved you because of your faith in Christ.
Your salvation doesn't come from anything you do.
It is God's gift.

EPHESIANS 2:8 NIRV

If you openly declare that Jesus is Lord and believe
in your heart that God raised him from the dead,
you will be saved.

ROMANS 10:9 NLT

God, may I never lose the wonder of the beautiful truth of salvation. May I forever be astonished that you would sacrifice your perfect Son, your deeply beloved, for me. You've made it so easy, Father. Just one thing you ask of me: believe. How can that be the only price? It's too good. You are too good. I praise you for my salvation.

How do you respond to the message of salvation?

Serving

Each of you should use whatever gift you have received
to serve others, as faithful stewards of God's grace in its
various forms. If anyone serves, they should do so with
the strength God provides, so that in all things God may
be praised through Jesus Christ.

1 PETER 4:10-11 NIV

Always give yourselves fully to the work of the Lord,
because you know that your labor in the Lord
is not in vain.

1 CORINTHIANS 15:58 NIV

You were called to freedom…do not use your freedom
as an opportunity for the flesh, but through love
serve one another.

GALATIANS 5:13 ESV

God, you are completely worthy of worship, yet you spend all your time thinking of others. Remake me in your image. Devotion to you looks like devotion to my brothers and sisters, and I want to give you all my allegiance. Give me a heart that is entirely focused on you and other people. Take away all thoughts of me, and replace them with expressions of you. I want to serve you and others before I serve myself.

Is there a way you can serve God and someone else today?

Strength

God is our refuge and strength,
an ever-present help in trouble.

PSALM 46:1-3 NIV

The Lord is faithful; he will strengthen you
and guard you from the evil one.

2 THESSALONIANS 3:3 NIRV

Don't be afraid, for I am with you.
Don't be discouraged, for I am your God.
I will strengthen you and help you.
I will hold you up with my victorious right hand.

ISAIAH 41:10 NLT

God is the strength of my heart
and my portion forever.

PSALM 73:26 NIV

Lord, your power knows no limits. When I think of how boundless your strength, how endless your ability, I stand in awe. Considering how easily I tire, how quickly I become overwhelmed, it is clear I am not calling on your power enough. With your help, exhaustion will not win. Spring up a well of energy in me. Allow me to finish strong so I can shout of your provision to all who hear.

What makes you feel strong?

Stress

Praise the LORD, my soul;
all my inmost being, praise his holy name.
Praise the LORD, my soul,
and forget not all his benefits—
who forgives all your sins
and heals all your diseases,
who redeems your life from the pit
and crowns you with love and compassion,
who satisfies your desires with good things
so that your youth is renewed like the eagle's.

PSALM 103:1-5 NIV

Commit your actions to the LORD.
and your plans will succeed.

PROVERBS 16:3 NLT

The LORD also will be a refuge... in times of trouble.

PSALM 9:9 NKJV

Wise God, can I sit awhile at your feet and rest? I like the sense of importance busyness gives me; I feel necessary, purposeful, and capable, but I've taken on so much I'm not sure I am capable, and my purpose has gotten a little unclear. Grant me perspective! I need to take time to replenish. Remind me I am important because you love me, not because of how much I get done.

When was the last time you were able to let go of stress and just sit with God?

Temptation

The temptations in your life are no different
from what others experience. And God is faithful.
He will not allow the temptation to be more than you
can stand. When you are tempted, he will show you
a way out so that you can endure.

1 CORINTHIANS 10:13 NLT

"Watch and pray so that you will not fall into temptation.
The spirit is willing, but the flesh is weak."

MATTHEW 26:41 NIV

I have taken your words to heart
so I would not sin against you.

PSALM 119:11 NCV

God, there is so much evil in this world. Every day a new danger, disaster, or form of depravity conspires to lure me from the peace of a life lived with you. It's tempting to give in, and sometimes I do. But this is not your way, and yours is the only way I want to lie. Deliver me to your perfect peace, that place where none of the temptations can touch me.

What temptations do you need to be delivered from today?

Thankfulness

I have not stopped giving thanks for you,
remembering you in my prayers.

EPHESIANS 1:16 NIV

Giving thanks is a sacrifice that truly honors me.
If you keep to my path, I will reveal to you
the salvation of God.

PSALM 50:23 NLT

Rejoice always, pray continually, give thanks
in all circumstances; for this is God's will for you
in Christ Jesus.

1 THESSALONIANS 5:16–18 NIV

Give thanks as you enter the gates of his temple.
Give praise as you enter its courtyards.
Give thanks to him and praise his name.

PSALM 100:4 NIRV

God, there is no end to your gifts. From the breath in my lungs to the roof over my head to every small mercy I receive today, you are a good gift giver. Thank you so much for the attention you pay to me every day. In every circumstance, I thank you.

What can you thank God for right now?

Trust

Those who know the LORD trust him,
because he will not leave those who come to him.

PSALM 9:10 NCV

I trust in you, LORD. I say, "You are my God."
My whole life is in your hands.
Save me from the hands of my enemies.
Save me from those who are chasing me.

PSALM 31:14-15 NIV

Yes, the LORD is for me; he will help me.
I will look in triumph at those who hate me.
It is better to take refuge in the LORD
than to trust in people.

PSALM 118:7-8 NLT

God, how is it that you always know what I need? How do you never tire of providing for me? I can count on you for the peace and joy I need to sustain me. What trust this inspires in my heart, and what gratitude! I know I don't deserve everything you give me, but that doesn't stop you. Your provision is as endless as your love. Thank you.

How do you know that God is trustworthy?

Truth

"When he, the Spirit of truth, comes,
he will guide you into all the truth."

JOHN 16:13 NIV

The very essence of your words is truth;
all your just regulations will stand forever.

PSALM 119:160 NLT

"If you abide in My word, you are My disciples indeed.
And you shall know the truth, and the truth
shall make you free."

JOHN 8:31-32 NKJV

Teach me your way, O LORD, that I may walk in your truth;
unite my heart to fear your name.

PSALM 86:11 ESV

God, you are truth. Everything you've said or done is honest, right, and good. Because you are truth, I want to value it as I value you. Point out the lies I tell myself, replacing them with truth. Stop me before a dishonest word leaves my mouth, giving me the most loving way to say instead what is true. Starting at this very moment, let me love the truth.

What steps can you take to be more truthful in your everyday life?

Understanding

Understanding is like a fountain of life
to those who have it.
But foolish people are punished
for the foolish things they do.

PROVERBS 16:22 NIRV

The teaching of your word gives light,
so even the simple can understand.

PSALM 119:130 NLT

Give me understanding,
so that I may keep your law
and obey it with all my heart.

PSALM 119:34 NIV

Don't act thoughtlessly, but understand
what the Lord wants you to do.

EPHESIANS 5:17 NLT

God, you are so wise! You always know what is right, and I need some of that wisdom for myself. When I rely on my own judgment, as I too often do, it's easy to get confused. Remind me what really matters, Lord, as I try to discern between your voice and others. Your will is the sweetest sound I know, and to know it is all I ask.

How do you seek to understand God's will each day?

Victory

You can prepare a horse for the day of battle.
But the power to win comes from the LORD.

Every child of God defeats this evil world,
and we achieve this victory through our faith.

1 JOHN 5:4 NLT

From the LORD comes deliverance.
May your blessing be on your people.

PSALM 3:8 NIV

"The LORD your God is the one who goes with you to fight
for you against your enemies to give you victory."

DEUTERONOMY 20:4 NIV

Lord, you are always with me. Any threat to my joy is an enemy of yours, which means it doesn't stand a chance. Thank you for being at the front of every battle I face. Thank you for your patience and gentle reassurance that the battle is already won. Victory is mine.

You win with Jesus in your life! Can you think of the last victory you experienced?

Wisdom

Wisdom will come into your mind,
and knowledge will be pleasing to you.
Good sense will protect you;
understanding will guard you
It will keep you from the wicked,
from those whose words are bad.

PROVERBS 2:10-12 NCV

Wisdom and money can get you almost anything,
but only wisdom can save your life.

ECCLESIASTES 7:12 NLT

If any of you needs wisdom, you should ask God for it.
He will give it to you. God gives freely to everyone
and doesn't find fault.

JAMES 1:5 NIRV

Wise and wonderful God, why do I look anywhere else for answers? Who besides you knows me so well, and loves me so completely? I have so many questions, and you have all the answers. I seek knowledge, goodness, and truth; you are these things. Grant me wisdom of my own. Most especially I pray for wisdom to go first and always to you: wisdom's only true source.

How can you use God's wisdom to make better choices?

Worry

Turn your worries over to the LORD.
He will keep you going.
He will never let godly people be shaken.

PSALM 55:22 NIRV

"Who of you by worrying can add
a single hour to your life?"

LUKE 12:25 NIV

Worry weighs a person down;
an encouraging word cheers a person up.

PROVERBS 12:25 NLT

Do not worry about anything, but pray and ask God for
everything you need, always giving thanks. And God's
peace, which is so great we cannot understand it,
will keep your hearts and minds in Christ Jesus.

PHILIPPIANS 4:6–7 NCV

Gracious God, because of you, I don't need to hold on to worry. Each time it rises up in me, I can come to you with my problems, laying my burdens at your feet, and you promise to help me. Even if you don't change my circumstances, you give me your peace so I can endure. Fill me now with your peace. Replace my worry with the assurance of your provision.

What worries can you hand over to God today?

BroadStreet Publishing® Group, LLC.
Savage, Minnesota, USA
Broadstreetpublishing.com

Amazing Grace: PRAYERS & PROMISES FOR WOMEN

© 2018 by BroadStreet Publishing

ISBN 978-1-4245-5859-9 (faux)
ISBN 978-1-4245-5491-1 (ebook)

Scripture quotations marked (NLT) are taken from the Holy Bible, New Living Translation, copyright © 1996, 2004, 2007. Used by permission of Tyndale House Publishers, Inc., Carol Stream, Illinois 60188. All rights reserved. Scripture quotations marked (NIV) are taken from the Holy Bible, New International Version®, NIV®. Copyright © 1973, 1978, 1984, 2011 by Biblica, Inc.™ Used by permission of Zondervan. All rights reserved worldwide. zondervan.com. The "NIV" and "New International Version" are trademarks registered in the United States Patent and Trademark Office by Biblica, Inc.™ Scripture quotations marked (NCV) are taken from the New Century Version®. Copyright © 2005 by Thomas Nelson. Used by permission. All rights reserved. Scripture quotations marked (NASB) are taken from the New American Standard Bible®, Copyright © 1960, 1962, 1963, 1968, 1971, 1972, 1973, 1975, 1977, 1995 by The Lockman Foundation. Used by permission. Lockman.org. Scripture quotations marked (NRSV) are taken from the New Revised Standard Version Bible, copyright 1989, Division of Christian Education of the National Council of the Churches of Christ in the United States of America. Used by permission. All rights reserved. Scripture quotations marked (ESV) are from the ESV® Bible (The Holy Bible, English Standard Version®), copyright © 2001 by Crossway, a publishing ministry of Good News Publishers. Used by permission. All rights reserved. Scripture quotations marked (TLB) are taken from The Living Bible copyright © 1971. Used by permission of Tyndale House Publishers, Inc., Carol Stream, Illinois 60188. All rights reserved. Scripture quotations marked (NKJV) are taken from the New King James Version®. Copyright © 1982 by Thomas Nelson. Used by permission. All rights reserved. Scripture quotations marked (NIRV) are taken from the Holy Bible, New International Reader's Version®, NIRV® Copyright © 1995, 1996, 1998, 2014 by Biblica, Inc.™ Used by permission of Zondervan. All rights reserved worldwide. www.zondervan.com The "NIRV" and "New International Reader's Version" are trademarks registered in the United States Patent and Trademark Office by Biblica, Inc.™.

Design by Chris Garborg | garborgdesign.com
Compiled and edited by Michelle Winger.

Printed in China.

17 18 19 20 21 22 23   7 6 5 4 3 2 1